Life Of David W. Patten

The First Apostolic Martyr

by

Lycurgus A. Wilson

LIFE OF DAVID W. PATTEN
THE FIRST APOSTOLIC MARTYR
by LYCURGUS A. WILSON

ISBN: 978-93-59323-67-1

Published by

DOUBLE 9 BOOKS

2/13-B, Ansari Road, Daryaganj
New Delhi – 110002
info@double9books.com
www.double9books.com
Tel. 011-40042856

ABOUT THE AUTHOR

Lycurgus A. Wilson was a dedicated author and historian known for his work "Life of David W. Patten. " Born in 1850, he lived during a crucial period of growth and development in The Church of Jesus Christ of Latter-day Saints (LDS Church) and contributed significantly to the documentation of the faith's history. Wilson's book, "Life of David W. Patten, " focuses on the life and contributions of David W. Patten, an important early leader in the LDS Church. Patten was one of the original members of the Quorum of the Twelve Apostles and played a vital role in the early expansion of Mormonism. In his biography, Lycurgus A. Wilson meticulously researched Patten's life, from his conversion to the LDS faith to his missionary work and eventual martyrdom. The book offers readers a detailed account of Patten's dedication to his religious beliefs and his unwavering commitment to the principles of Mormonism. One of the highlights of the biography is its portrayal of Patten's involvement in significant events, such as the Zion's Camp expedition and his role as a missionary and apostle. Wilson's work serves as an important historical record, providing insights into the challenges and triumphs experienced by early Latter-day Saints.

CONTENTS

PREFACE

The writing of this little volume has been a pleasant task. And just as we find mingled with our regret at parting with a friend, a joy in the assurance that to whomsoever he comes he will give the same pleasure he has afforded us, so the author has a feeling in putting out this brief memoir of David W. Patten that the courage and faith manifested in his life will not be lost or unfruitful in the lives of those who contemplate his career.

There remains only the pleasure of thanking those who have taken an interest in this work, and their name is legion. But first of all perhaps is the nephew of Apostle Patten, Thomas Jefferson Patten, of Provo, Utah.

Particular mention should be made of the kindness shown by the late President Wilford Woodruff, by President Lorenzo Snow, by President Joseph F. Smith, by the late Apostle Franklin D. Richards and by the late President Abraham O. Smoot, of Utah Stake. In short, all who knew, or who have read of, Apostle David W. Patten, have seemed to count it a pleasure to do whatever they could to assist in perpetuating his memory.

L.A.W.

Salt Lake City, Utah,
February 8, 1900.

CHAPTER I

Early life of David W. Patten — Parentage — Marriage — Joins the Methodists — Learns of the restoration of the Gospel — Visits his brother — Resume of Church history — Receives Baptism — First mission.

Great men are the Lord's object lessons to the world. They hold out to mankind the measure of truth committed to their generation. As example is greater than precept, so a life may state a truth more forcibly than words.

When He answered the question as to the first great commandment, the Savior did more than satisfy the idle curiosity of the listening crowd, he indicated one of the underlying purposes of this life and stated the principle by which the degree of civilization will be determined.

Measured by the love he bore his Maker and his fellow-men, few greater men have ever lived than David Wyman Patten. With all the intensity of his nature, he served the Lord, and with the same undivided purpose he was devoted to the welfare of humanity. Having in mind that divine precept, "Greater love hath no man than this, that a man lay down his life for his friend," the Prophet Joseph Smith said over the remains of this great Apostle, "There lies a man who has done just as he said he would — he has laid down his life for his friends."

Of David's early life little is known. While he was quite young, his parents, Benenio Patten and Abagail Cole Patten, removed from the State of Vermont, where he was born about the year 1800, to the town of Theresa, at Indian River Falls, in the western part of the State of New York.

Leaving home while yet a boy, he made his way to the southeastern part of Michigan, and made himself a home in the woods a short distance above the little town of Dundee, in Monroe County, where he married Miss Phoebe Ann Babcock, in 1828. Here, too, though telling his fellow-religionists that there was no true religion on the earth, he allied himself with the Methodists.

Having been from youth of a religious turn of mind, he had received a particular manifestation of the Holy Ghost when he was twenty-one years of age. Being admonished to humble himself before the Lord and repent of his sins, he enjoyed for the next three years a close communion with the Lord, through visions and dreams of the night. In one of these it was made known to him that the Church of Christ would be established in his day, and he looked forward to such an event with joyous anticipation.

When about the age of twenty-four years, as he tells us in his meager journal, he became, through the cares of the world, neglectful in conduct, and remained so to some extent until he was thirty years old, when, by sincere repentance, he again received a testimony that his sins were forgiven. Under these conditions and at about this time he saw for the first time a copy of the Book of Mormon, but only long enough to read the inspired preface and the testimony of the eleven witnesses. From this time he prayed continually for faith and a more perfect knowledge. It was while living in anticipation of just such an event, therefore, that he received, in the latter part of May, 1832, a letter from his elder brother, John Patten, of Fairplay, Indiana, informing him of the restoration of the Gospel.

The message fairly caused his heart to leap for joy. He seemed conscious of the light which was about to burst upon him. He knew by intuition that his life's darkness was over, and that henceforward he should walk in the light of eternal truth. He arose in the meeting that day—for it was on a Sunday he received the intelligence—and told the assembly that he had at last got word of the Church of Christ.

Impatient to be off, he mounted his old grey mare the next morning and started alone through the woods on a journey of three hundred miles. That part of the country in those days was little more than a wilderness. The roads by which the settlers had come from their eastern homes ran, in the main, east and west, so that David's way to the south led him over hills, through valleys and across rivers by paths almost unknown to the white man; but nature was in her glory, the birds made melody the day through, and, more than all else, his own heart, swelling with gratitude, kept time to the music of the spheres, for God had again spoken from the heavens, the questionings of his soul since boyhood had been answered, and those paths, rough though they were, led to the realization of his highest hopes this side of eternity. That otherwise lonely journey was filled with peace and happiness unspeakable.

Arrived at the home of his brother, at Fairplay, he found him, before an infidel, now a devoted Christian and substantially as the history of the rise of the Church was related to him we shall repeat it here:

"In a little town six hundred miles to the east, in the State of New York, a young man named Joseph Smith, while praying in the woods twelve years ago, received a visit from God the Father and His Son Jesus Christ. Three years later, an angel, calling himself Moroni, appeared to this youth and explained that he was a resurrected being who had formerly lived on this continent in the flesh. Telling the boy Joseph of a sacred record hidden in a hill near by, the angel met him on the hillside where the precious charge lay concealed in a stone box, and after repeated admonitions during the four subsequent years, delivered to him some gold plates and an instrument called a Urim and Thummim, with which to translate the inspired hieroglyphics.

"After much delay and a great deal of persecution, the youth succeeded in reproducing from the gold plates the record known as the Book of Mormon, now published to the world these three years.

"Two years and two months ago, having received authority under the hands of John the Baptist, as also from Peter, James and John, the ancient apostles, this modern Prophet, in accordance with directions from the Lord, organized the true Church of Christ, at Fayette, Seneca County, in the State of New York.

"The next fall after the Church was set up, three missionaries came west with the intention of introducing the work among the Indians, who are descended from an ancient people of whom the Book of Mormon gives the history; and on their way came among an earnest body of worshippers at Kirtland, Ohio. These read the book, believed the testimony, and received baptism to the number of several hundred souls.

"Receiving a visit from a number of these converts, the Prophet himself has removed with his family to Kirtland, where he now lives with a number of his followers.

"It has, moreover, been revealed to the Prophet that the ancient site of the Garden of Eden is on this continent, and that the building of the New Jerusalem is to commence at that sacred spot. Accordingly, the converts to the new faith are gathering from all directions into Independence, Missouri, where about four hundred of them are now settled."

Interesting as this narrative is to us, though we have heard it for the hundredth time, how much more interesting must it have been to David W. Patten, for it was all new to him. Drinking it in with his whole soul, he received the truth with joy, and was led into the waters of baptism on the 15th day of June, 1832.

With the most of men there is lingering in the very heart of their faith a grain of doubt. Even the missionary, no doubt, feels easier in placing himself in the hands of the Lord, when he knows that if no place is furnished him to sleep, he can with the dollar in his pocket provide for himself. And so it is with each of us at times. It seems as though we cannot free ourselves from the millstone of doubt, and take the Lord at His word when He says He will provide for those who trust Him. This was not the case, however, with David W. Patten. He stood six feet and one inch in height, and weighed over two hundred pounds; but there seems to have been no room in his whole generous composition for a particle of doubt. He took the Lord at His word and devoted his whole life to His service; and whether face to face with Cain, or baring his breast to an infuriated mob, a doubt that the Lord was with him seems thenceforth never to have entered his mind.

Two days after his baptism David was ordained an Elder under the hands of Elisha H. Groves, and with Joseph Wood, another recent convert, as a companion, was given a mission to the Territory of Michigan.

CHAPTER II

His procedure in administering to the sick — Testimony as to his success — Visits the Prophet — Missionary labors — Casts out a "devil" — His family baptized — Mrs. Strong healed — Called to Jackson County.

Those who have had a like experience, will know with what joy the new convert returned to his friends in the wilderness. All business was laid aside. With his companion, David traveled through all the country round about preaching the Gospel and healing the sick.

Immediately upon taking up his labors in Michigan, in calling at the house of a stranger to ask for dinner, David found in the family a very sick child, and while discussing the restoration of the Gospel with the parents, was asked to administer to the little one. Finding the mother had faith, he did so, and it was at once healed.

In administering the healing ordinance David had a method of procedure peculiarly his own. On reaching the beside, he would first teach the principles of the Gospel and bear his testimony to their truth, when he usually made a promise that the invalid should be healed if he would agree to accept baptism. President Abraham O. Smoot, of Utah Stake, once said he never knew an instance in which David's petition for the sick was not answered, and this was also the testimony of President Wilford Woodruff.

At the close of one of his meetings in Michigan, where he had no doubt spoken of the gift of healing, two children sick of fever and ague were brought to the meeting-house to be healed. David had started off, but was called back and upon learning from the parents of their faith, acceded to their request, and the children were healed instantly.

Until the latter part of September David and his companion labored in Southeastern Michigan, baptizing sixteen persons in a branch of the Maumee River during that time. Late in the summer they took up a journey to Kirtland, preaching by the way.

Perhaps the first person they met at Kirtland was Elder Joseph C. Kingsbury, for they inquired of him at Newel K. Whitney's store the way to the home of the Prophet Joseph. It was early in October; the Prophet was on a mission east, and while waiting his return, David spent the next two or three weeks on the Prophet's farm, helping to dig potatoes and harvest corn.

Soon after the return of the Prophet Joseph Smith, David W. Patten was sent into Pennsylvania on his second mission, traveling sometimes with John Murdock as a companion, and at other times with Reynolds Cahoon.

The Prophet, in sending out these early missionaries, had no particular field of labor in mind for any of them. They were sent to warn all men, but their message was specially to the honest in heart, and these they had no way of finding except by the inspiration of the Lord. Just at this time a large number of Elders had been sent east from Kirtland in response to the revelation of September 22, 1832, from which we quote as follows:

> "62. Go ye into all the world, and whatsoever place ye cannot go into ye shall send, that the testimony may go from you into all the world unto every creature.

> "63. And as I said unto mine apostles, even so I say unto you, for you are mine apostles, even God's High Priests; ye are they whom my Father hath given me — ye are my friends;

> "64. Therefore, as I said unto mine apostles I say unto you again, that every soul who believeth on your words, and is baptized by water for the remission of sins, shall receive the Holy Ghost;

> "65. And these signs shall follow them that believe.

> "66. In my name they shall do many wonderful works;

> "67. In my name they shall cast out devils;

> "68. In my name they shall heal the sick;

> "69. In my name they shall open the eyes of the blind, and unstop the ears of the deaf;

> "70. And the tongue of the dumb shall speak;

> "71. And if any man shall administer poison unto them it shall not hurt them;

> "72. And the poison of a serpent shall not have power to harm them.

> "73. But a commandment I give unto them, that they shall not boast themselves of these things, neither speak them before the world, for these things are given unto you for your profit and for salvation.

> "74. Verily, verily, I say unto you they who believe not on your words, and are not baptized in water, in my name, for the remission of their sins, that they may receive the Holy Ghost, shall be damned, and shall not come into my Father's kingdom, where my Father and I am.

"75. And this revelation unto you, and commandment, is in force from this very hour upon all the world, and the gospel is unto all who have not received it.

"76. But, verily, I say unto all those to whom the kingdom has been given, from you it must be preached unto them, that they shall repent of their former evil works, for they are to be upbraided for their evil hearts of unbelief; and your brethren in Zion for their rebellion against you at the time I sent you.

"77. And again I say unto you, my friends, (for from henceforth I shall call you friends,) it is expedient that I give unto you this commandment, that ye become even as my friends in days when I was with them traveling to preach the gospel in my power,

"78. For I suffered them not to have purse or scrip, neither two coats;

"79. Behold I send you out to prove the world, and the laborer is worthy of his hire.

"80. And any man that shall go and preach this gospel of the kingdom, and fail not to continue faithful in all things shall not be weary in mind, neither darkened, neither in body, limb, nor joint: and an hair on his head shall not fall to the ground unnoticed. And they shall not go hungry, neither athirst.

"81. Therefore, take no thought for the morrow, for what ye shall eat, or what ye shall drink, or wherewithal ye shall be clothed;

"82. For consider the lilies of the field, how they grow, they toil not, neither do they spin; and the kingdoms of the world, in all their glory, are not arrayed like one of these;

"83. For your Father who art in heaven, knoweth that you have need of all these things.

"84. Therefore, let the morrow take thought for the things of itself.

"85. Neither take ye thought beforehand what ye shall say, but treasure up in your minds continually the words of life, and it shall be given you in the very hour that portion that shall be meted unto every man.

"86. Therefore let no man among you, (for this commandment is unto all the faithful who are called of God in the church unto the ministry,) from this hour take purse or scrip, that goeth forth to proclaim this gospel of the kingdom.

"87. Behold, I send you out to reprove the world of all their unrighteous deeds, and to teach them of a judgment which is to come.

"88. And whoso receiveth you, there I will be also, for I will go before your face: I will be on your right hand and on your left, and my Spirit shall be in your hearts, and mine angels round about you, to bear you up.

"89. Whoso receiveth you receiveth me, and the same will feed you, and clothe you, and give you money.

"90. And he who feeds you, or clothes you or gives you money, shall in no wise lose his reward:

"91. And he that doeth not these things is not my disciple; by this you may know my disciples.

"92. He that receiveth you not, go away from him alone by yourselves, and cleanse your feet even with water, pure water, whether in heat or in cold, and bear testimony of it unto your Father which is in heaven, and return not again unto that man.

"93. And in whatsoever village or city ye enter, do likewise.

"94. Nevertheless, search diligently and spare not; and wo unto that house, or that village or city that rejecteth you, or your words, or your testimony concerning me.

"95. Wo, I say again, unto that house, or that village or city that rejecteth you, or your words, or your testimony of me.

"96. For I the Almighty, have laid my hands upon the nations, to scourge them for their wickedness:

"97. And plagues shall go forth, and they shall not be taken from the earth until I have completed my work which shall be cut short in righteousness,

"98. Until all shall know me, who remain, even from the least unto the greatest, and shall be filled with the knowledge of the Lord, and shall see eye to eye, and shall lift up their voice, and with the voice together sing this new song, saying—

"99. The Lord hath brought again Zion; The Lord hath redeemed his people, Israel, According to the election of grace, Which was brought to pass by the faith And covenant of their fathers.

"100. The Lord hath redeemed his people, And Satan is bound and time is no longer: The Lord hath gathered all things in one: The Lord hath brought down Zion from above. The Lord hath brought up Zion from beneath.

"101. The earth hath travailed and brought forth her strength: And truth is established in her bowels: And the heavens have smiled upon her: And she is clothed with the glory of her God: For he stands in the midst of his people:

"102. Glory, and honor, and power, and might, Be ascribed to our God; for he is full of mercy, Justice, grace and truth, and peace, For ever and ever, Amen.

"103. And again, verily, verily I say unto you, it is expedient that every man who goes forth to proclaim mine everlasting gospel, that inasmuch as they have families, and receive monies by gift that they should send it unto them or make use of it for their benefit, as the Lord shall direct them, for thus it seemeth me good.

"104. And let all those who have not families, who receive monies, send it up unto the Bishop in Zion, or unto the Bishop in Ohio, that it may be consecrated for the bringing forth of the revelations and the printing thereof, and for establishing Zion.

"105. And if any man shall give unto any of you a coat, or a suit, take the old and cast it unto the poor, and go your way rejoicing.

"106. And if any man among you be strong in the Spirit, let him take with him he that is weak, that he may be edified in all meekness, that he may become strong also.

"107. Therefore, take with you those who are ordained unto the lesser priesthood, and send them before you to make appointments, and to prepare the way, and to fill appointments that you yourselves are not able to fill.

"108. Behold, this is the way that mine apostles, in ancient days, built up my church unto me.

"109. Therefore, let every man stand in his own office, and labor in his own calling; and let not the head say unto the feet, it hath no need of the feet, for without the feet how shall the body be able to stand?

"110. Also the body hath need of every member, that all may be edified together, that the system may be kept perfect.

"111. And behold the High Priests should travel, and also the elders, and also the lesser priests; but the deacons and teachers should be appointed to watch over the church, to be standing ministers unto the church.

"112. And the bishop, Newel K. Whitney, also, should travel round about and among all the churches, searching after the poor to administer to their wants by humbling the rich and the proud;

"113. He should also employ an agent to take charge and to do his secular business as he shall direct.

"114. Nevertheless, let the bishop go unto the city of New York, also to the city of Albany, and also to the city of Boston, and warn the people of those cities with the sound of the gospel, with a loud voice, of the desolation and utter abolishment which await them if they do reject these things;

"115. For if they do reject these things the hour of their judgment is nigh, and their house shall be left unto them desolate.

"116. Let him trust in me and he shall not be confounded; and an hair of his head shall not fall to the ground unnoticed.

"117. And verily I say unto you, the rest of my servants, go ye forth as your circumstances shall permit, in your several callings unto the great and notable cities and villages, reproving the world in righteousness of all their unrighteous and ungodly deeds, setting forth clearly and understandingly the desolation of abomination in the last days.

"118. For with you saith the Lord Almighty, I will rend their kingdoms: I will not only shake the earth, but the starry heavens shall tremble;

"119. For I, the Lord, have put forth my hand to exert the powers of heaven; ye cannot see it now, yet a little while and ye shall see it, and know that I am, and that I will come and reign with my people.

"120. I am Alpha and Omega, the beginning and the end. Amen." — Doc. and Cov. Sec. 84.

On the 9th of November, in eastern Ohio, David fell in with John F. Boynton and Zebedee Coltrin, who like himself were uncertain as to their course, and the three thereupon held a council of inquiry. Agreeing that Zebedee Coltrin should be mouth, the three went into a wood near by and knelt in prayer. They were directed to go eastward, preaching as they went. This they did, and David adds, "the Spirit of God leading us." Several persons were baptized on their way.

At Springfield, Pa., David met Hyrum Smith and his brother William, and joined them in holding services. After meeting, six persons were baptized. David's gift of healing the sick was in constant demand. People came to him from all the country round, and it was a dally occurrence for the sick to be healed under his administrations. One woman, who had been an invalid for twenty years, was healed instantly.

After four months' labor in and about Pennsylvania, David returned to Kirtland, arriving there February 25, 1833.

David was a man of great physical strength. While on his third mission, which was undertaken after a month's rest at Kirtland, he and Reynolds Cahoon had an appointment to preach at the house of Father Bosley, at Avon, Ohio.

Several meetings had been held here before by other Elders, and among the assembled neighbors, was a man known as the "County Bully," who was the source of a great deal of annoyance to the speakers.

Sitting by the door in the hallway, this man would, every little while, contradict the speaker, or call out some irreverent suggestion, or ask for a sign. He boisterously refused to be quiet, and on the evening of David's meeting at the house, was particularly noisy, asking David, among other things, to cast the devil out. Whether it was from a sense of humor at the fellow's unlucky remark, or because he was tired of the disturbance, we cannot say, but David finally determined to silence his persecutor.

Walking to the hallway, he quietly picked the man up bodily, carried him to the outside door, and with a swing sent the fellow about ten feet onto the wood pile. There was no more disturbance that night, and the saying was the current mirth provoker of the neighborhood for weeks afterward, that "Patten cast out one devil, soul and body."

While on this mission, David assisted in converting a part of his own family. On the 20th of May, 1833, at Theresa, Indian River Falls, his brothers, Archibald and Ira, his sister Polly, his mother, and two of his brothers-in-law, Warren Parrish and Mr. Cheeseman, were led into the waters of baptism by Elder Brigham Young, who was another of the large number of missionaries sent out from Kirtland in March, 1833. David's father had died in August the previous year.

For nearly a year now David had been almost continuously in the field, preaching the Gospel and healing the sick, his power with the Lord in no wise diminishing. No credit was ever taken to himself, however, in the miracles performed, for he writes of this time:

"The Lord did work with me wonderfully, in signs and wonders following them that believed in the fulness of the Gospel of Jesus Christ, insomuch that the deaf were made to hear, the blind to see, and the lame were made whole. Fevers, palsies, crooked and withered limbs, and in fact all manner of diseases common to the country, were healed by the power of God, that was manifested through his servants."

Among those visited by him was a blind woman, the wife of Ezra Strong. It was nearly noon when David reached the house. After the usual testimony and questions respecting her faith in the Gospel, David rubbed and anointed her eyes, when immediately she was restored to sight; and so thoroughly was she healed that she prepared dinner for the household.

During this summer, under great hardship and suffering, eighty members were added to the Church under David's administration. Eighteen of these were at Orleans, Jefferson County, New York. At Henderson where eight converts were baptized, great power was manifested at the confirmation, when the members spoke in tongues and prophesied.

With his brother, Ira, David returned in the early autumn of 1833 to Kirtland, where he worked on the temple for a month. Before winter set in that year, David had removed his wife and their effects from Michigan to Florence, Ohio, where he remained till the latter part of November. Having been sickly, five weeks of the seven he spent at home that fall, David commended himself into the hands of the Lord and went into the neighboring country to preach. But there was a field more in need of his labors than this, for he had not been from home more than two weeks when the word of the Lord came to him as follows:

"Depart from your field of labor, and go unto Kirtland, for behold, I will send thee up to the land of Zion, for behold, thou shalt serve thy brethren there."

CHAPTER III

Condition of Saints in Missouri—Revelation to them—With William D. Pratt, David goes to Missouri—Ministering to the suffering—Freedom from animosity—Mission to Tennessee—Healing of Mrs. Lane.

Greatly were his brethren in Zion in need of whatever services David could render them. About the time of his arrival at Kirtland after receiving the word of the Lord, a letter came to the Prophet from Elder W. W. Phelps, dated Clay County, Missouri, in which among other things he says:

"The situation of the Saints, as scattered, is dubious and affords a gloomy prospect. No regular order can be enforced, nor any usual discipline kept up; among the world, yea, among the most wicked part of it, some commit one sin and some another (I speak of the rebellious, for there are Saints that are as immovable as the everlasting hills,) and what can be done? We are in Clay, Ray, Lafayette, Jackson, Van Buren, etc., and cannot hear from each other oftener than we do from you.

"I know it was right that we should be driven out of the land of Zion, that the rebellious might be sent away. But, brethren, if the Lord will, I should like to know what the honest in heart shall do."

On December 16th, 1833, the Lord gave, in answer to this inquiry, the following revelation:

"1. Verily I say unto you, concerning your brethren who have been afflicted, and persecuted, and cast out from the land of their inheritance,

"2. I, the Lord, have suffered the affliction to come upon them, wherewith they have been afflicted, in consequence of their transgressions;

"3. Yet I will own them, and they shall be mine in that day when I shall come to make up my jewels.

"4. Therefore, they must needs be chastened and tried, even as Abraham, who was commanded to offer up his only son;

"5. For all those who will not endure chastening, but deny me, cannot be sanctified.

"6. Behold, I say unto you, there were jarrings, and contentions, and envyings, and strifes, and lustful and covetous desires among them; therefore by these things they polluted their inheritances.

"7. They were slow to hearken unto the voice of the Lord their God, therefore the Lord their God is slow to hearken unto their prayers, to answer them in the day of their trouble.

"8. In the day of their peace they esteemed lightly my counsel; but, in the day of their trouble, of necessity they feel after me.

"9. Verily, I say unto you, notwithstanding their sins, my bowels are filled with compassion towards them: I will not utterly cast them off; and in the day of wrath I will remember mercy.

"10. I have sworn, and the decree hath gone forth by a former commandment which I have given unto you, that I would let fall the sword of mine indignation in the behalf of my people; and even as I have said, it shall come to pass.

"11. Mine indignation is soon to be poured out without measure upon all nations, and this will I do when the cup of their iniquity is full.

"12. And in that day all who are found upon the watch tower, or in other words, all mine Israel shall be saved.

"13. And they that have been scattered shall be gathered;

"14. And all they who have mourned shall be comforted;

"15. And all they who have given their lives for my name shall be crowned.

"16. Therefore, let your hearts be comforted concerning Zion; for all flesh is in mine hands: be still and know that I am God.

"17. Zion shall not be moved out of her place, notwithstanding her children are scattered;

"18. They that remain, and are pure in heart, shall return, and come to their inheritances, they and their children, with songs of everlasting joy to build up the waste places of Zion;

"19. And all these things that the prophets might be fulfilled.

"20. And, behold, there is none other place appointed than that which I have appointed; neither shall there be any other place appointed than that which I have appointed, for the work of the gathering of my saints,

"21. Until the day cometh when there is found no more room for them; and then I have other places which I will appoint unto them, and they shall be called Stakes, for the curtains, or the strength of Zion.

"22. Behold, it is my will, that all they who call on my name, and worship me according to mine everlasting gospel, should gather together, and stand in holy places,

"23. And prepare for the revelation which is to come, when the veil of the covering of my temple, in my tabernacle, which hideth the earth, shall be taken off, and all flesh shall see me together.

"24. And every corruptible thing, both of man, or of the beasts of the field, or of the fowls of the heavens, or of the fish of the sea, that dwell upon all the face of the earth, shall be consumed;

"25. And also that of element shall melt with fervent heat; and all things shall become new, that my knowledge and glory may dwell upon all the earth.

"26. And in that day the enmity of man, and the enmity of beasts, yea, the enmity of all flesh, shall cease from before my face.

"27. And in that day whatsoever any man shall ask, it shall be given unto him.

"28. And in that day Satan shall not have power to tempt any man.

"29. And there shall be no sorrow because there is no death.

"30. In that day an infant shall not die until he is old, and his life shall be as the age of a tree.

"31. And when he dies he shall not sleep, (that is to say in the earth,) but shall be changed in the twinkling of an eye, and shall be caught up, and his rest shall be glorious.

"32. Yea, verily I say unto you, in that day when the Lord shall come, he shall reveal all things—

"33. Things which have passed, and hidden things which no man knew—things of the earth, by which it was made, and the purposes, and the end thereof—

"34. Things most precious—things that are above, and things that are beneath—things that are in the earth, and upon the earth, and in heaven.

"35. And all they who suffer persecution for my name, and endure in faith, though they are called to lay down their lives for my sake, yet shall they partake of all this glory.

"36. Wherefore, fear not even unto death; for in this world your joy is not full, but in me your joy is full.

"37. Therefore, care not for the body, neither the life of the body; but care for the soul, and for the life of the soul;

"38. And seek the face of the Lord always, that in patience ye may possess your souls, and ye shall have eternal life.

"39. When men are called unto mine everlasting gospel, and covenant with an everlasting covenant, they are accounted as the salt of the earth, and the savor of men;

"40. They are called to be the savor of men. Therefore, if that salt of the earth lose its savor, behold, it is thenceforth good for nothing, only to be cast out, and trodden under the feet of men.

"41. Behold, here is wisdom concerning the children of Zion, even many, but not all; they were found transgressors, therefore they must needs be chastened.

"42. He that exalteth himself shall be abased, and he that abaseth himself shall be exalted.

"43. And now, I will show unto you a parable, that you may know my will concerning the redemption of Zion.

"44. A certain nobleman had a spot of land, very choice; and he said unto his servants, Go ye unto my vineyard, even upon this very choice piece of land, and plant twelve olive trees,

"45. And set watchmen round about them, and build a tower, that one may overlook the land round about, to be a watchman upon the tower, that mine olive trees may not be broken down, when the enemy shall come to spoil, and take unto themselves the fruit of my vineyard.

"46. Now, the servants of the nobleman went and did as their lord commanded them; and planted the olive trees, and built a hedge round about, and set watchmen, and began to build a tower.

"47. And while they were yet laying the foundation thereof, they began to say among themselves, And what need hath my lord of this tower?

"48. And consulted for a long time, saying among themselves, What need hath my lord of this tower, seeing this is a time of peace?

"49. Might not this money be given to the exchangers? for there is no need of these things!

"50. And while they were at variance one with another they became very slothful, and they hearkened not unto the commandments of their lord,

"51. And the enemy came by night, and broke down the hedge, and the servants of the nobleman arose and were affrighted, and fled; and the enemy destroyed their works, and broke down the olive trees.

"52. Now behold, the nobleman, the lord of the vineyard, called upon his servants, and said unto them, Why! what is the cause of this great evil?

"53. Ought ye not to have done even as I commanded you? and after ye had planted the vineyard, and built the hedge round about, and set watchmen upon the walls thereof, built the tower also, and set a watchman upon the tower, and watched for my vineyard, and not have fallen asleep, lest the enemy should come upon you?

"54. And behold, the watchman upon the tower would have seen the enemy while he was yet afar off, and then ye could have made ready and kept the enemy from breaking down the hedge thereof, and saved my vineyard from the hands of the destroyer.

"55. And the lord of the vineyard said unto one of his servants, Go and gather together the residue of my servants, and take all the strength of mine house, which are my warriors, my young men, and they that are of middle age also among all my servants, who are the strength of mine house, save those only whom I have appointed to tarry;

"56. And go ye straightway unto the land of my vineyard, and redeem my vineyard, for it is mine, I have bought it with money.

"57. Therefore, get ye straightway unto my land; break down the walls of mine enemies; throw down their tower, and scatter their watchmen:

"58. And inasmuch as they gather together against you, avenge me of mine enemies, that by and by I may come with the residue of mine house, and possess the land.

"59. And the servant said unto his lord, When shall these things be?

"60. And he said unto his servant, When I will, go ye straightway, and do all things whatsoever I have commanded you;

"61. And this shall be my seal and blessing upon you — a faithful and wise steward in the midst of mine house, a ruler in my kingdom.

"62. And his servant went straightway, and did all things whatsoever his lord commanded him, and after many days all things were fulfilled.

"63. Again, verily I say unto you, I will show unto you wisdom in me concerning all the churches, inasmuch as they are willing to be guided in a right and proper way for their salvation,

"64. That the work of the gathering together of my saints may continue, that I may build them up unto my name upon holy places; for the time of harvest is come, and my word must needs be fulfilled.

"65. Therefore, I must gather together my people, according to the parable of the wheat and the tares, that the wheat may be secured in the garners to possess eternal life, and be crowned with celestial glory when I shall come in the kingdom of my Father, to reward every man according as his work shall be,

"66. While the tares shall be bound in bundles, and their bands made strong, that they may be burned with an unquenchable fire.

"67. Therefore, a commandment I give unto all the churches, that they shall continue to gather together unto the places which I have appointed;

"68. Nevertheless, as I have said unto you in a former commandment, let not your gathering be in haste, nor by flight; but let all things be prepared before you:

"69. And in order that all things be prepared before you, observe the commandments which I have given concerning these things,

"70. Which saith, or teacheth, to purchase all the lands by money, which can be purchased for money, in the region round about the land which I have appointed to be the land of Zion, for the beginning of the gathering of my saints;

"71. All the land which can be purchased in Jackson County, and the counties round about, and leave the residue in mine hand.

"72. Now, verily I say unto you, let all the churches gather together all their monies; let these things be done in their time, be not in haste, and observe to have all things prepared before you.

"73. And let honorable men be appointed, even wise men, and send them to purchase these lands;

"74. And every church in the eastern countries when they are built up, if they will hearken unto this counsel, they may buy lands and gather together upon them, and in this way they may establish Zion.

"75. There is even now already in store a sufficient, yea, even abundance, to redeem Zion, and establish her waste places, no more to be thrown down, where the churches who call themselves after my name, willing to hearken to my voice.

"76. And again I say unto you, those who have been scattered by their enemies, it is my will that they should continue to importune for redress, and redemption, by the hands of those who are placed as rulers, and are in authority over you.

"77. According to the laws and constitution of the people which I have suffered to be established, and should be maintained for the rights and protection of all flesh, according to just and holy principles,

"78. That every man may act in doctrine and principle pertaining to futurity, according to the moral agency which I have given unto them, that every man may be accountable for his own sins in the day of judgement.

"79. Therefore, it is not right that any man should be in bondage one to another.

"80. And for this purpose have I established the constitution of this land, by the hands of wise men whom I raised up unto this very purpose, and redeemed the land by the shedding of blood.

"81. Now, unto what shall I liken the children of Zion? I will liken them unto the parable of the woman and the unjust judge (for men ought always to pray and not to faint) which saith,

"82. There was in a city a judge which feared not God, neither regarded man.

"83. And there was a widow in that city, and she came unto him, saying, Avenge me of mine adversary.

"84. And he would not for a while, but afterward he said within himself, Though I fear not God, nor regard man, yet because this widow troubleth me I will avenge her, lest, by her continual coming, she weary me.

"85. Thus will I liken the children of Zion.

"86. Let them importune at the feet of the Judge;

"87. And if he heed them not, let them importune at the feet of the Governor;

"88. And if the Governor heed them not, let them importune at the feet of the President;

"89. And if the President heed them not, then will the Lord arise and come forth out of his hiding place, and in his fury vex the nation,

"90. And in his hot displeasure, and in his fierce anger, in his time, will cut off those wicked, unfaithful, and unjust stewards, and appoint them their portion among hypocrites, and unbelievers;

"91. Even in outer darkness, where there is weeping and wailing, and gnashing of teeth.

"92. Pray ye, therefore, that their ears may be opened unto your cries, that I may be merciful unto them, that these things may not come upon them.

"93. What I have said unto you, must needs be, that all men may be left without excuse;

"94. That wise men and rulers may hear and know that which they have never considered;

"95. That I may proceed to bring to pass my act, my strange act, and perform my work, my strange work, that men may discern between the righteous and the wicked, saith your God.

"96. And again, I say unto you, it is contrary to my commandment, and my will, that my servant Sidney Gilbert should sell my storehouse, which I have appointed unto my people, into the hands of mine enemies.

"97. Let not that which I have appointed be polluted by mine enemies, by the consent of those who call themselves after my name;

"98. For this is a very sore and grievous sin against me, and against my people, in consequence of those things which I have decreed and are soon to befall the nations.

"99. Therefore, it is my will that my people should claim, and hold claim upon that which I have appointed unto them, though they should not be permitted to dwell thereon;

"100. Nevertheless, I do not say they shall not dwell thereon; for inasmuch as they bring forth fruit and works meet for my kingdom, they shall dwell thereon;

"101. They shall build, and another shall not inherit it; they shall plant vineyards, and they shall eat the fruit thereof. Even so. Amen." — Doc. and Cov. Sec. 101.

With a copy of this revelation and other papers bearing comfort to the distressed people, David accompanied William D. Pratt to Missouri, making the greater part of the journey on foot.

Under date of December 19th occurs the following entry in the diary of the Prophet Joseph Smith:

"William Pratt and David Patten took their journey to the land of Zion, for the purpose of beating dispatches to the brethren in that place from Kirtland. O, may God grant it a blessing for Zion, as a kind angel from heaven. Amen."

To face that journey of six hundred miles in the dead of winter on foot and in poverty, took no common courage. Men who weighed their own comfort against the welfare of their fellowmen, would have seriously considered the alternative. But not so with these.

Since the summer of 1831, when the Saints first settled in Jackson County, Missouri, converts had been gathering from all parts of the country to the center Stake of Zion. Much progress had been made by them in providing themselves with the comforts of life, when, in the fall of 1833, an armed mob recruited from the surrounding region arose against the Saints and drove them, about twelve hundred souls in all, from their homes, and now they were as we have seen scattered and in distress.

After much suffering on this perilous journey, David reached Clay County, where his brother John had located, on March 24, 1834. He found the Saints in a truly pitiable condition. Driven from their homes in and about Independence before the crops of the previous year could be utilized, their fields laid waste, their houses and in many instances all their belongings burned by the mob, many of the people hardly knew how they had been preserved through the winter. The Lord only will ever know.

David's whole soul went out to the sufferers. His time was spent night and day in ministering to their necessities. That attribute of the Lord, which we are sent here particularly to cultivate, of love for all things, was most fully exercised in David during this period of his development. Even the most despised of the animal kingdom came within the reach of his sympathy, for while traveling among the people he interposed whenever opportunity offered to prevent the destruction even of the rattlesnakes with which the country was infested. Explaining on one such occasion that we need not look for animals to become harmless so long as men cherish enmity, he drove the intruder with a brush of leaves into retirement.

Not even the men who had brought upon his brethren and sisters the suffering he so untiringly sought to relieve, could call from David any heated demonstration of bitterness. While he stood ready to go with the Saints back to their homes, and advocated such a course, he was yet unwilling to entertain for their enemies a feeling of vengeance.

In June, 1834, when Zion's camp had arrived, David met in council with a number of his brethren and the leaders of the mob. At the close of the conference, on account of some remark of his, one of the mobocrats drew a bowie knife on David, swearing:

"You d—d Mormon, I'll cut your d—d throat."

"My friend, do nothing rash."

"For God's sake don't shoot."

David's composure and gentle reply threw the man into a state of alarm for his own safety. It was beyond him to conceive of such unruffled demeanor unless his antagonist relied for his security on concealed weapons. But David was wholly unarmed, except with the affection which knows no fear. There are other instances in his career when David's fearlessness led his enemies to believe he was armed. These, however, will be noted as we proceed.

The Prophet Joseph left Missouri for Kirtland early in July, and in September David took a steamer at the small town of La Grange on the Mississippi river, and, in company with Warren Parrish, started on a mission to the Southern States. At Paris, Henry County, Tennessee, where they arrived in October, the Elders remained preaching about three months. During this time twenty converts were made and many sick were healed.

Of the many cases of healing performed under David's administrations, one of the most wonderful perhaps was that of the wife of Johnston F. Lane. She had been sick for eight years, and for a year past had been unable to walk. Hearing of the Elders she begged her husband to send for them. David answered the summons at once. As was his custom, he first explained the Gospel and upon receiving from the lady an assurance of faith in the Lord, he laid his hands on her, saying:

"In the name of Jesus Christ, I rebuke the disorder and command it to depart."

As he said this she was instantly made whole, and at his command and in accordance with her promise, she went into the water and was baptized within the hour. Among the promises made her at her confirmation, was one that she should bear a son in less than a year, though she had been married twelve years and was childless. The prophecy was fulfilled, and, out of gratitude to the servant of the Lord under whose hands the mother had been so marvelously healed, the child was named David Patten Lane. The mother bore several children afterward.

CHAPTER IV

Chosen an Apostle—Ordination—Revelation instructing the Twelve—Date of birth—Healing of Mrs. Stearns—Impression of Lorenzo Snow.

From Paris, Tennessee, David made his way to Kirtland, where events very nearly concerning him were soon to take place.

Even before the organization of the Church, two of the witnesses to the Book of Mormon, were directed to search out the Twelve Apostles, and as a mark by which these men were to be known the Lord particularizes:

"And the Twelve are they who shall desire to take upon them my name with full purpose of heart."

In his diary under date of 1835, the Prophet Joseph writes:

"On the Sabbath previous to the 14th of February, Brothers Joseph and Brigham Young came to my house after meeting and sang for me; the Spirit of the Lord was poured out upon us, and I told them I wanted those brethren together who went up to Zion in the camp the previous summer, for I had a blessing for them."

Of the minutes of that meeting on February 14th, a brief extract will be interesting:

"President Joseph Smith, Jr., after making many remarks on the subject of choosing the Twelve, wanted an expression from the brethren if they would be satisfied to have the Spirit of the Lord dictate in the choice of the Elders to be Apostles; whereupon all the Elders present expressed their anxious desire to have it so.

"A hymn was then sung, 'Hark, Listen to the Trumpeters.' President Hyrum prayed and the meeting was dismissed for one hour.

"Assembled pursuant to adjournment, and commenced with prayer.

"President Joseph Smith, Jr., said that the first business of the meeting was for the three witnesses of the Book of Mormon to pray, each one, and then proceed to choose twelve men from the Church as Apostles, to go to all nations, kindreds, tongues and people.

"The three witnesses, viz., Oliver Cowdery, David Whitmer and Martin Harris, united in prayer.

"These three witnesses were then blessed by the laying on of the hands of the Presidency.

"The witnesses then, according to a former commandment, proceeded to make a choice of the Twelve. Their names are as follows:

Lyman E. Johnson,
Brigham Young,
Heber C. Kimball,
Orson Hyde,
David W. Patten,
Luke Johnson,
Wm. E. McLellin,
John F. Boynton,
Orson Pratt,
William Smith,
Thos. B. Marsh,
Parley P. Pratt."

Under the hands of the witnesses, the Twelve were next ordained. David's ordination occurred on Sunday, February 15, 1835, in language of which the following quotation from the minutes is probably only a synopsis:

"O God, give this, Thy servant, a knowledge of Thy will; may he be like one of old, who bore testimony of Jesus; may he be a new man from this day forth. He shall be equal with his brethren, the Twelve, and have the qualifications of the Prophets before him; may his body be strong and never weary; may he walk and not faint. May he have power over all diseases, and faith according to his desires; may the heavens be opened upon him speedily, that he may bear testimony from knowledge; that he may go to the nations and isles afar off. May he have a knowledge of the things of the kingdom from the beginning, and be able to tear down priestcraft like a lion; may he have power to smite his enemies before him with utter destruction; may he continue till the Lord comes. O Father, we seal these blessings upon him. Even so. Amen."

The period intervening till the 4th of May, when their first mission was entered upon, was a veritable Pentecost to the newly chosen Twelve. Through the Prophet Joseph and his counselors the Lord truly poured out upon them the choicest blessings of heaven. On March 28th, in answer to their petition for "a revelation of His mind and will concerning our duty the coming season, even a great revelation that will enlarge our hearts, comfort us in adversity, and brighten our hopes amidst the powers of darkness," the

Lord, through the Prophet, answered every desire of their hearts with the revelation Section 107, in the Doctrine and Covenants, as follows:

"1. There are in the church, two Priesthoods, namely, the Melchisedek, and Aaronic, including the Levitical priesthood.

"2. Why the first is called the Melchisedek Priesthood, is because Melchisedek was such a great High Priest.

"3. Before his day it was called the Holy Priesthood, after the order of the Son of God;

"4. But out of respect or reverence to the name of the Supreme Being, to avoid the too frequent repetition of his name, they, the church, in ancient days, called that Priesthood after Melchisedek, or the Melchisedek Priesthood.

"5. All other authorities or offices in the church are appendages to this Priesthood.

"6. But there are two divisions or grand heads—one is the Melchisedek Priesthood, and the other is the Aaronic, or Levitical Priesthood.

"7. The office of an Elder comes under the Priesthood of Melchisedek.

"8. The Melchisedek Priesthood holds the right of Presidency, and has power and authority over all the offices in the church in all ages of the world, to administer in spiritual things.

"9. The Presidency of the High Priesthood, after the order of Melchisedek, have a right to officiate in all the offices in the church.

"10. High Priests after the order of the Melchisedek Priesthood, have a right to officiate in their own standing, under the direction of the Presidency, in administering spiritual things; and also in the office of an elder, priest, (of the Levitical order,) teacher, deacon, and member.

"11. An elder has a right to officiate in his stead when the High Priest is not present.

"12. The High Priest and elder are to administer in spiritual things, agreeable to the covenants and commandments of the church; and they have a right to officiate in all these offices of the church when there are no higher authorities present.

"13. The second priesthood is called the priesthood of Aaron, because it was conferred upon Aaron and his seed, throughout all their generations.

"14. Why it is called the lesser priesthood, is because it is an appendage to the greater or the Melchisedek Priesthood, and has power in administering outward ordinances.

"15. The bishopric is the presidency of this priesthood and holds the keys or authority of the same.

"16. No man has a legal right to this office, to hold the keys of this priesthood, except he be a literal descendant of Aaron.

"17. But as a High Priest of the Melchisedek Priesthood has authority to officiate in all the lesser offices, he may officiate in the office of bishop when no literal descendant of Aaron can be found, provided he is called and set apart and ordained unto this power by the hands of the Presidency of the Melchisedek Priesthood.

"18. The power and authority of the Higher or Melchisedek Priesthood, is to hold the keys of all the spiritual blessings of the church—

"19. To have the privilege of receiving the mysteries of the kingdom of heaven—to have the heavens opened unto them—to commune with the general assembly and church of the first born, and to enjoy the communion and presence of God the Father, and Jesus the Mediator of the new covenant.

"20. The power and authority of the lesser, or Aaronic priesthood, is to hold the keys of the ministering of angels, and to administer in outward ordinances, the letter of the gospel—the baptism of repentance for the remission of sins, agreeable to the covenants and commandments.

"21. Of necessity there are presidents, or presiding offices growing out of, or appointed of or from among those who are ordained to the several offices in these two priesthoods.

"22. Of the Melchisedek Priesthood, three Presiding High Priests, chosen by the body, appointed and ordained to that office, and upheld by the confidence, faith, and prayer of the church, form a quorum of the Presidency of the church.

"23. The Twelve traveling counselors are called to be the Twelve Apostles, or special witnesses of the name of Christ in all the world; thus differing from other officers in the church in the duties of their calling.

"24. And they form a quorum, equal in authority and power to the three Presidents previously mentioned.

"25. The seventy are also called to preach the gospel, and to be especial witnesses unto the Gentiles and in all the world. Thus differing from other officers in the church in the duties of their calling;

"26. And they form a quorum equal in authority to that of the Twelve special witnesses or apostles just named.

"27. And every decision made by either of these quorums, must be by the unanimous voice of the same; that is, every member in each quorum must be agreed to its decisions, in order to make their decisions of the same power or validity one with the other.

"28. (A majority may form a quorum, when circumstances render it impossible to be otherwise.)

"29. Unless this is the case, their decisions are not entitled to the same blessings which the decisions of a quorum of three Presidents were anciently, who were ordained after the order of Melchisedek, and were righteous and holy men.

"30. The decisions of these quorums, or either of them, are to be made in all righteousness, in holiness, and lowliness of heart, meekness and long-suffering, and in faith, and virtue, and knowledge, temperance, patience, godliness, brotherly kindness and charity;

"31. Because the promise is, if these things abound in them, they shall not be unfruitful in the knowledge of the Lord.

"32. And in case that any decision of these quorums is made in unrighteousness, it may be brought before a general assembly of the several quorums, which constitute the spiritual authorities of the church, otherwise there can be no appeal from their decision.

"33. The Twelve are a traveling presiding High Council, to officiate in the name of the Lord, under the direction of the Presidency of the church, agreeable to the institution of heaven; to build up the church, and regulate all the affairs of the same in all nations; first unto the Gentiles, and secondly unto the Jews.

"34. The seventy are to act in the name of the Lord, under the direction of the Twelve or the traveling High Council, in building up the church and regulating all the affairs of the same in all nations—first unto the Gentiles and then to the Jews;

"35. The Twelve being sent out, holding the keys to open the door by the proclamation of the gospel of Jesus Christ—and first unto the Gentiles and then unto the Jews.

"36. The standing High Councils, at the Stakes of Zion, form a quorum equal in authority, in the affairs of the church, in all their decisions, to the quorum of the Presidency, or to the traveling High Council.

"37. The High Council in Zion, form a quorum equal in authority, in the affairs of the church, in all their decisions, to the Councils of the Twelve at the Stakes of Zion.

"38. It is the duty of the traveling High Council to call upon the seventy, when they need assistance, to fill the several calls for preaching and administering the gospel, instead of any others.

"39. It is the duty of the Twelve, in all large branches of the church, to ordain evangelical ministers, as they shall be designated unto them by revelation.

"40. The order of this Priesthood was confirmed to be handed down from father to son, and rightly belongs to the literal descendants of the chosen seed, to whom the promises were made.

"41. This order was instituted in the days of Adam, and came down by lineage in the following manner: —

"42. From Adam to Seth, who was ordained by Adam at the age of 69 years, and was blessed by him three years previous to his (Adam's) death, and received the promise of God by his father that his posterity should be the chosen of the Lord, and that they should be preserved unto the end of the earth,

"43. Because he (Seth) was a perfect man, and his likeness was the express likeness of his father's, insomuch that he seemed to be like unto his father in all things, and could be distinguished from him only by his age.

"44. Enos was ordained at the age of 134 years and four months, by the hand of Adam.

"45. God called upon Cainan in the wilderness, in the fortieth year of his age, and he met Adam in journeying to the place Shedolamak. He was 87 years old when he received his ordination.

"46. Mahalaleel was 496 years and seven days old when he was ordained by the hand of Adam, who also blessed him.

"47. Jared was 200 years old when he was ordained under the hand of Adam, who also blessed him.

"48. Enoch was 25 years old when he was ordained under the hand of Adam, and he was 65 and Adam blessed him.

"49. And he saw the Lord, and he walked with him, and was before his face continually; and he walked with God 365 years, making him 430 years old when he was translated.

"50. Methuselah was 100 years old when he was ordained under the hand of Adam.

"51. Lamech was 32 years old when he was ordained under the hand of Seth.

"52. Noah was 10 years old when he was ordained under the hand of Methuselah.

"53. Three years previous to the death of Adam, he called Seth, Enos, Cainan, Mahalaleel, Jared, Enoch, and Methuselah, who were all High Priests, with the residue of his posterity who were righteous, into the valley of Adam-ondi-Ahman, and there bestowed upon them his last blessing.

"54. And the Lord appeared unto them, and they rose up and blessed Adam, and called him Michael, the Prince, the Archangel.

"55. And the Lord administered comfort unto Adam and said unto him, I have set thee to be at the head—a multitude of nations shall come of thee, and thou art a prince over them for ever.

"56. And Adam stood up in the midst of the congregation, and notwithstanding he was bowed down with age, being full of the Holy Ghost, predicted whatsoever should befall his posterity unto the latest generation.

"57. These things were all written in the book of Enoch, and are to be testified of in due time.

"58. It is the duty of the Twelve, also, to ordain and set in order all the other officers of the church."

Just before starting off on their first mission as a quorum unto the eastern states, to set the branches of the Church in order, the Twelve were instructed to take their places in council, according to age, the oldest to be seated at the head. In pursuance thereof, the Twelve were arranged with Thomas B. Marsh, David W. Patten and Brigham Young in the order named; and this fact gives us the most definite information we now have as to the date of David's birth. Thomas B. Marsh, being the oldest of the Twelve, was born November 1, 1799, and Brigham Young on June 1, 1801, and somewhere between these dates was the birthday of David.

The 4th of May saw the departure of the Twelve from Kirtland. The next five months were spent by David in traveling with his quorum through New York, Canada, Vermont, and Maine, holding meetings and setting branches in order.

While a conference was being held at Bethel, Maine, a young woman, Mary Ann Stearns, who had been troubled for five years with an extremely aggravated case of heart disease, sent for the Elders, and upon investigation asked for baptism. David was mouth in the confirmation as well as in administering to her afterward for her health, and made her the promise that she should be entirely restored to perfect health and soundness. She afterwards became the wife of Apostle Parley P. Pratt, and endured all the hardships through which the Saints were called to pass; but from that time till the time of her death in 1891, at the age of eighty-two years, she never again complained of heart trouble.

The Twelve returned to Kirtland in September, 1835.

The indelibility of the impressions made by David upon those with whom he associated was something remarkable. Though it is more than sixty years since his death, the Saints who knew him in life still recall with pleasure the inspiration of his presence. In the course of a ride of twenty-five miles with him on horseback about the time of David's return from his mission with the Twelve, Lorenzo Snow first received a testimony of the truth of the Gospel. Sister Eliza R. Snow in the biography of her brother best describes the occurrence:

"On his way to Oberlin, my brother accidentally fell in company with David W. Patten, an incident to which he frequently refers as one of those seemingly trivial occurrences in human life which leaves an indelible trace. This gentleman was an early champion of the fulness of the Gospel as taught by Jesus and his Apostles in the meridian of time, and revealed in our own day through the Prophet Joseph Smith, to which cause Elder Patten fell a martyr on the 24th of October, 1838, in Missouri, during the terrible scenes of persecution through which the Latter-day Saints passed in that State. He possessed a mind of deep thought and rich intelligence. In conversation with him, my brother was much impressed with the depth and beauty of the philosophical reasoning with which this inspired Elder seemed perfectly familiar as he descanted on the condition of the human family in connection with the sayings of the ancient Prophets, as recorded in the Scriptures — the dealings with, and the purposes of God in relation to, His children on the earth. From that time a new field with a new train of reflections, was open to my brother's mind, the impress of which has never been erased."

CHAPTER V

A period of rest — Endowments — Second mission to Tennessee — Meets Wilford Woodruff and Abraham O. Smoot — Trial by mob court — Escape — Interview with Cain — Bares his breast to a mob.

Without doubt the most enjoyable period of David's life, was that spent at home with his wife, and in council with his Quorum, in Kirtland, during the next eight months. Mingling with his brethren in the most intimate relationship, in the school for the study of languages, in the school of the Prophets, each preparing himself in mutual bearing and forbearance one with another, to receive his endowments at the dedication of the Temple, David won from all their lasting love and respect.

At the dedication of the Kirtland Temple on March 27, 1836, after giving the interpretation of a discourse in tongues delivered by Brigham Young, David himself spoke in tongues.

Receiving his blessings and endowments in the Temple directly after its dedication, David took his wife and started on another mission into Tennessee, where he met for the first time Wilford Woodruff and Abraham O. Smoot.

Of this time President Woodruff writes:

"Brother Smoot traveled with me constantly till the 21st of April, when he had the privilege of meeting with Elder David W. Patten, who had come direct from Kirtland, and who had been ordained one of the Twelve Apostles.

"It was a happy meeting. He gave us an account of the endowments at Kirtland, the glorious blessings received, the ministration of angels, the organization of the Twelve Apostles and Seventies, and informed me that I was appointed a member of the second quorum of Seventies. All of this was glorious news to me, and caused my heart to rejoice.

"On the 27th of May we were joined by Elder Warren Parrish, direct from Kirtland. We had a happy time together.

"On the 28th, we held a conference at Brother Seth Utley's, where were represented all the branches of the Church in the South.

"I was ordained on the 31st of May a member of the second quorum of Seventies under the hands of David W. Patten and Warren Parrish.

"At the close of the conference we separated for a short time. Elders Patten and Parrish labored in Tennessee, Brother Smoot and myself in Kentucky. On the 9th of June we all met at Damon Creek Branch, where Brother Patten baptized two. One was Father Henry Thomas, who had been a revolutionary soldier under General Washington, and father of Daniel and Henry Thomas.

"A warrant was issued, on the oath of a priest, against D. W. Patten, W. Parrish and myself. We were accused in the warrant of the great 'crime' of testifying that Christ would come in this generation, and that we promised the Holy Ghost to those whom we baptized. Brothers Patten and Parrish were taken on the 19th of June. I being in another county, escaped being arrested. The brethren were put under two thousand dollars bonds to appear at court. Albert Petty and Seth Utley were their bondsmen.

"They were tried on the 22nd of June.

"They plead their own cause. Although men came forward and testified they did receive the Holy Ghost after they were baptized, the brethren were condemned; but were finally released by paying the expenses of the mob court.

"There was one peculiar circumstance connected with this trial by a mob court, which was armed to the teeth. When the trial was through with, the people were not willing to permit more than one to speak. Warren Parrish had said but few words, and they were not willing to let David Patten speak. But he, feeling the injustice of the court, and being filled with the power of God, arose to his feet and delivered a speech of about twenty minutes, holding them spell-bound while he told them of their wickedness and the abominations that they were guilty of, also of the curse of God that awaited them, if they did not repent, for taking up two harmless, inoffensive men for preaching the Gospel of Christ.

"When he had got through his speech the judge said, 'You must be armed with secret weapons, or you would not talk in this fearless manner to an armed court.'

"Brother Patten replied: 'I have weapons that you know not of, and they are given me of God, for He gives me all the power I have.'

"The judge seemed willing to get rid of them almost upon any terms, and offered to dismiss them if their friends would pay the costs, which the brethren present freely offered to do.

"When the two were released, they mounted their horses and rode a mile to Seth Utley's; but, as soon as they had left, the court became ashamed that they had been let go so easily and the whole mob mounted their horses to follow them to Utley's.

"One of the Saints, seeing the state of affairs, rode on before the mob to notify the brethren, so that they had time to ride into the woods near by.

"They traveled along about three miles to Brother Albert Petty's, and went to bed. The night was dark, and they fell asleep.

"But Brother Patten was warned in a dream to get up and flee, as the mob would soon be there. They both arose, saddled their animals, and rode into the adjoining county.

"The house they had just left was soon surrounded by the mob, but the brethren had escaped through the mercy of God."

In that expression, referring to the Lord, "He gives me all the power I have," Apostle David W. Patten gave at once the secret and the watchword of his wonderful career.

It was probably not long after his arrival in Tennessee in the spring of 1836, that David had one of the most remarkable experiences of his life. He was making his home with Levi Taylor, the stepfather of Abraham O. Smoot, at the time and had been to Paris, some sixteen miles away, holding a meeting. Riding home in the evening, just where his road lay through a dense growth of brush, called in those parts a "barren," he suddenly became aware that a person on foot by his side was keeping pace with the mule on which he rode.

But the subjoined letter, dated at Provo, Utah, will explain the matter:

President Joseph F. Smith, Salt Lake City:

Dear Brother:—In relation to the subject of the visit of Cain to Brother David W. Patten in the State of Tennessee, about which you wrote to me, I will say that according to the best of my recollection it was in the month of September, 1835.

It was in the evening, just twilight, when Brother Patten rode up to my father's house, alighted from his mule and came into the house. The family immediately observed that his countenance was quite changed. My mother having first noticed his changed appearance said: "Brother Patten, are you sick?" He replied that he was not, but had just met with a very remarkable personage who had represented himself as being Cain, who murdered his brother, Abel. He went on to tell the circumstances as near as I can recall in the following language:

> "As I was riding along the road on my mule I suddenly noticed a very strange personage walking beside me. He walked along beside me for about two miles. His head was about even with my shoulders as I sat in my saddle. He wore no clothing, but was covered with hair. His skin was very dark. I asked him where he dwelt and he replied that he had no home, that he was a wanderer in the earth and traveled to and fro. He said he was a very miserable creature, that he had earnestly sought death during his sojourn upon the earth, but that he could not die, and his mission was to destroy the souls of men. About the time he expressed himself thus, I rebuked him in the name of the Lord Jesus Christ and by virtue of the Holy Priesthood, and commanded him to go hence, and he immediately departed out of my sight. When he left me I found myself near your house."

There was much conversation about the circumstances between Brother Patten and my family which I don't recall, but the above is in substance his statement to us at the time. The date is, to the best of my recollection, and I think it is correct, but it may possibly have been in the spring of 1836, but I feel quite positive that the former date is right.

Hoping the above will be satisfactory to you and answer your purpose, I am with the kindest regards, as ever,

Your friend and Brother,

A. O. Smoot.

Another incident showing David's utter fearlessness, occurred about this time. While preaching at the house of Father Fry, in Benton county,

Tennessee, David was interrupted by a Mr. Rose, who asked him to raise the dead. David administered to the man a stinging rebuke for his wickedness, when Mr. Rose in great anger left the house. After meeting, however, he returned, bringing with him a crowd of armed men, who stood in sullen array about the dooryard.

Probably for the reason that he did not wish the family to be disturbed by them, David went out, cane in hand, to learn their intentions. He was greeted with the brandishing of weapons and dire threats of vengeance; but with the utmost coolness he bared his breast to the mob, and told them to shoot. The same fear seemed to fall upon them that possessed the mobocrat in Missouri, for they fled the premises as if in fear of their lives.

David had now arrived at the state of advancement, noticeable alike in the life of the Saviour, and in the closing years of the Prophet Joseph, where one sees, in the light of eternal truth, the utter shallowness and worthlessness of worldly pride and pretense, and, cognizant of the fact that no amount of tolerance will cure the evil, is moved to awaken humility with a sharp rebuke.

That evening, President Woodruff relates, he and David went to a stream of clear water below the house, and washed their hands and feet as the Lord directs, and bore testimony against those wicked men.

CHAPTER VI

David's personal appearance—Healing of Abraham O. Smoot—
Margaret Tittle healed—Prophecy at Paris, Tennessee—Journey
to Far West—Visits Kirtland during the great apostasy—Chosen
to Presidency in Missouri—Revelation—Expresses a wish to die
as a martyr.

Probably the description of David's personal appearance with which the most of those who knew him in life agree, is that given by President Abraham O. Smoot, who says he was about six feet one inch in height, stoutly built, though not fleshy, and of a dark complexion, with piercing black eyes. As to disposition, President Smoot describes him as jovial, qualifying his expression, however, with the closing remark:

"His jokes, though, were pretty solid."

At one time while traveling with David, Abraham O. Smoot, then little more than a boy, became so sick he could sit on his horse no longer. Stopping at the house of an atheist, Brother Smoot was put to bed, and David assisted their hostess to prepare the sick man some warm drinks.

His companion receiving no relief, David obtained permission to "attend prayers," and kneeling down by the bedside he laid his hands upon the sick man's head and asked the Lord to heal him.

"Every bit of pain left me," said Brother Smoot, in relating the incident, "in the twinkling of an eye."

It was just following this remark that President Smoot said:

"I don't recollect that he ever failed in his importuning to heal the sick."

Once, when David and Wilford Woodruff were traveling together, they were called to the bedside of a sick woman, Margaret Tittle, who lay at the point of death. Preaching the Gospel to her, David received a promise that if healed she would be baptized. After being administered to by the servants of the Lord, she was restored to perfect health instantly, when she refused baptism.

They told her she was acting a dangerous part and would again be attacked if she did not repent. Returning that way in a few days, they found her very low again, when she again promised, but this time with more sincerity, for after being healed the second time, she was led into the water and baptized, by Wilford Woodruff.

On August 20th, David preached at the house of Randolph Alexander, and after meeting baptized him and his wife.

The spirit of mobocracy seemed always to have aroused in David all the resentment of which he was capable. At one time while holding a meeting in Pads, Tennessee, as related by President Woodruff, a mob gathered in the place of meeting with threats of violence. Instead, however, of being intimidated by their presence, David denounced their undertaking in the most unmeasured terms and in the spirit of prophecy, though the fulfillment in the Civil War was then more than twenty-five years away, predicted:

"Before you die some of you will see the streets of Paris run with the blood of its own citizens."

How fearfully this prophecy was fulfilled in the capture of Paris in 1862 by General Morgan, during his famous raid through Kentucky and Tennessee!

Early in September, the seven branches of the Church in Kentucky and Tennessee, representing one hundred and thirty-three members, assembled in conference on Damon's Creek, Calloway County, Kentucky, Thomas B. Marsh, as President of the Twelve Apostles, presiding. On the third day of the conference, David preached on repentance and baptism, and at the close of the meeting, five persons came forward and asked to be baptized.

Directly after conference, David with his wife took leave of the Saints and his fellow laborers, and returned in safety with Thomas B. Marsh and companion, Elisha H. Groves, to Missouri.

In leaving the field of his labors of the past six months, in company with Elisha H. Groves, who had first conferred upon him authority to enter the missionary field, it was but natural that David should retrospectively contemplate the work to which his life had been so wholly given over since that lonely ride through the woods from Michigan to Indiana. His first disappointing missionary labors among his friends and acquaintances in Michigan, when he expected all of them to rejoice with him in the great light newly burst upon the world; the first visit to the Prophet Joseph, followed by the two successive missions in the East; his winter's journey with William D. Pratt; his labors in Missouri and in the South; his ordination to the Apostleship with the wonderful feast of blessings and endowments that followed; the return to the South, just terminated all these reflections crowded upon him with all their accompanying memories of toil and privation, with all the accompanying memories of the powers and blessings the Lord had bestowed upon him; and there was no room in his soul for anything but gratitude. Not only so, but there was a more settled resolution to persevere to the end; and it was probably on this journey back to Missouri that in David's mind the nature of that end was predetermined.

Upon his return to Missouri, after an absence of two years, David found not a few marks of progress in the condition of the Saints. A new town had been laid out called Far West, into which the people were gathering from every quarter. Efforts were being made to purchase all the land in the newly created County of Caldwell, and it was to gather means for this purpose that President Thomas B. Marsh had made his recent visit into Kentucky.

Locating on a single lot in the northwest part of town given him by the Saints, David soon had a plain log house erected, and from that time he devoted himself entirely to the welfare of the Church. His zeal in spreading the truth abroad, was not surpassed by that manifested in its defense at home.

Early in the spring of 1837, David preferred charges before the High Council in Zion against Lyman Wight for teaching false doctrine. At the trial in Far West on April 24th the charges were sustained, the proper acknowledgements soon after accepted by the Saints and harmony restored. The incident illustrates the disinterestedness and manliness of David's character, for his action in this matter seems only to have drawn closer the ties of confidence and friendship existing between himself and his commanding officer in the militia, Colonel Lyman Wight.

In June, in company with Thomas B. Marsh and William D. Pratt, David, responding to a call for a meeting of the Twelve, took a mission through the intervening States to Kirtland, where they arrived in the midst of the great apostasy. Here was need of all the courage he could command, for it was a time to test the integrity of the strongest.

Deception and fraud and darkness had overcome his close friend and brother-in-law, Warren Parrish, who tried by every means in his power to turn David himself against the Prophet; and the downfall of his brethren at that time was one of the greatest sorrows of David's life. Not long after the conference at Kirtland in September, 1837, David returned to Far West.

The spirit of the apostasy soon spreading into Missouri, it was found necessary to displace the three Presidents, David Whitmer, John Whitmer and W. W. Phelps. In consequence, Thomas B. Marsh and David W. Patten were, on February 10th, sustained as temporary Presidents of the Church in Missouri, pending the arrival of the Prophet Joseph Smith from Kirtland. At the coming of the Prophet, March 14th, 1838, a conference was called, at which three weeks later, Thomas B. Marsh was chosen President in Missouri, and David W. Patten and Brigham Young his assistants.

Shortly after, on April 17, 1838, the following revelation was received through the Prophet Joseph Smith:

> "1. Verily thus said the Lord, it is wisdom in my servant David W. Patten, that he settle up all his business as soon as he possibly can, and make a disposition of his merchandise, that he may perform a mission unto me next spring, in company with others, even Twelve, including himself, to testify of my name, and bear glad tidings unto the world.
>
> "2. For verily thus saith the Lord, that inasmuch as there are those among you who deny my name, others shall be planted in their stead, and receive bishopric. Amen." — Doc. and Cov. Sec. 114.

It was probably this revelation that occasioned a conversation between the Prophet and David, reported by Wilford Woodruff.

David made known to the Prophet that he had asked the Lord to let him die the death of a martyr, at which the Prophet, greatly moved, expressed extreme sorrow, "for," said he to David, "when a man of your faith asks the Lord for anything, he generally gets it."

CHAPTER VII

Visits Adam-ondi-Ahman—Address to the Saints—Spirit of mobocracy in Missouri—David known as "Captain Fear Not"—Calms a storm—Mobocracy and treason—David succeeds to the Presidency of Twelve.

In May, David left Far West with the Prophet Joseph and party to lay off a Stake of Zion to the north of them. It was on this trip that Adam's altar was discovered, at Adam-ondi-Ahman, where a revelation was given through the Prophet as follows:

"1. Adam-ondi-Ahman, because, said he, it is a place where Adam shall come to visit his people, or the Ancient of Days shall sit, as spoken of by Daniel the Prophet."—Doc. and Cov. Sec. 116.

In his official capacity, David issued an epistle to the Saints through the Elder's Journal, under date of July, 1838, into which, notwithstanding the imperfect typography as here copied, there is breathed a spirit of concern for the welfare of the people of God, equalled only by that of integrity in defense of the Prophet Joseph Smith.

To the Saints abroad:

Dear Brethren and Sisters: Whereas, many have taken into hand to set forth the order of the Kingdom of God on earth, and have testified of the grace of God, as given unto them, to publish unto you, I also feel it my duty to write unto you, touching the grace of God given unto me, to youward; concerning the dispensation we have received; which is the greatest of all dispensations— And has been spoken of by the mouths of all the holy prophets since the word began. In this, my communication to you, I design to notice some of these prophecies. Now the Apostle Paul says on this wise, "For I would not, brethren, that you should be ignorant of this mystery, (lest you should be wise in your own conceit), that blindness in part has happened unto Israel, until the fulness of the Gentiles be come in. And so all Israel shall be saved; as is written. There shall come out of Zion a deliverer, and shall turn away ungodliness from Jacob." What is that he says? "For I would not have you ignorant." Ignorant of what? Why of this mystery, that blindness in part had happened unto Israel. And to what end? Why, that salvation might come unto the

Gentiles. — See the 12th and 13th verses of this chapter (11) to the Romans. Now if the fall of them be the riches of the world, and the diminishing of them the riches of the Gentiles; how much more their fulness? "For I speak to you Gentiles, inasmuch as I am the apostle to the Gentiles, I magnify mine office." Now, we are to understand the apostle, as speaking of the return of Israel, when he said "how much more their fulness," in their return. "For I would not have you ignorant concerning this matter," that blindness will depart, from them in the day that the fulness of the Gentiles is come in, and the reason is very obvious, because it is said, that out of Zion shall come the deliverer; and for what cause? Why that the word of God might be fulfilled. This deliverer might, through the mercy of God, turn away ungodliness from Jacob. This work evidently commences at the time God begins to take the darkness from the minds of Israel, for this will be the work of God by the deliverer, for he shall turn away ungodliness from the whole family of Jacob. "For this is my covenant with them, when I shall take away their sins." Now them, we can see that this deliverer is a kind of harbinger or forerunner, that is, one that is sent to prepare the way for another. And this deliverer is such a one, for he comes to turn away ungodliness from Jacob. Consequently he must receive a dispensation and authority suitable to his calling, or he could not turn away ungodliness from Jacob, nor fulfill the scripture. But the words of the prophets must be fulfilled. And in order to do this, to this messenger must be given the dispensation of the fulness of times according to the prophets. For Paul says again, in speaking of the dispensation of the fulness of times; Ephesians 1, 9: "Having made known unto us the mystery of his will according to his good pleasure, which he has purposed in himself, that in the dispensation of the fulness of times, he might gather together in one all things in Christ, both which are in Heaven and which are on earth, even in him." And Isaiah says in the 11th chapter and 11th verse, "And it shall come to pass in that day, that the Lord shall set his hand again the second time to recover the remnant of his people." Now, this is the time that the deliverer shall come out of Zion, and turn away ungodliness from the house of Israel.

Now the Lord has said that he would set his hand the second time and we ask for what? but to recover the house of Israel. From what have they fallen? most assuredly they had broken the covenant, that God had made with their fathers, and through their fathers with them.

For Paul says, Romans, 11: 19, 20: "Thou wilt say then, the branches were broken off, that I might be grafted in. Well, because of unbelief they were broken off, and thou standest by faith. Be not high minded, but fear."

Now it is evident, that the Jews did forsake the Lord, and by that means broke the covenant, and now we see the need of the Lord's setting his hand the second time to gather his people, according to Eph. 1:10, "That the dispensation of the fulness of times," etc. Now I ask, What is a dispensation? I answer, it is power and authority to dispense the word of God, and to administer in all the ordinances thereof. This is what we are to understand by it, for no man ever had the Holy Ghost to deliver the Gospel, or to prophesy of things to come, but had liberty to fulfill his mission; consequently, the argument is clear, for it proves itself; nevertheless, I will call on the scriptures to prove the assertion. Ephesians 3:2, "If ye have heard of the dispensation of the grace of God, which is given me to you ward. How that by revelation he made known unto me the mystery; as I wrote in a few words." And also in Colossians 1:25: "Wherefore I am made a minister, according to the dispensation of God which is given to me for you to fulfill the words of God." It is evident then, that the dispensation given the apostle, came to him by revelation from God. Then by this we may understand, in some degree, the power by which he spake, as also the dispensation of the fulness of times.

Now, this at first thought, would appear very small to some, who are not acquainted with the order of God from the beginning; but when we take into consideration the plan of God for the salvation of the world, we can readily see that plan carried out most faithfully in all its bearings. See after the fall of Adam, the plan of salvation was made known to him of God himself; who in like manner, in the meridian of time revealed the same, in sending his first begotten Son, Jesus Christ: who also revealed the same to the apostles, and God raised him from the dead to perfect that plan. And the apostles were made special witnesses of that plan; and testified that "in the dispensation of the fulness of times, that God would gather together in one, all things in Christ, whether they be things in Heaven, or things on earth." Now the thing to be known is, what the fulness of times means, or the extent and authority thereof. It means this, that the dispensation of the fulness of times is made up of all the dispensations that ever have been given since the world began until this time. Unto Adam first was given a dispensation. It is well known that God spake to him with his own voice in the garden, and gave him the promise of the Messiah. And unto Noah also was a dispensation given. For Jesus, said, "As it was in the days of Noah, so shall it be at the coming of the son of man." And as the righteous were saved then, and the wicked destroyed, so it will be now. And from Noah to Abraham; and from Abraham to Moses; and from Moses to Elias; and from Elias to John the Baptist; and from John to Jesus; and from Jesus to Peter, James and John. The apostles all having received in their time, a dispensation by revelation from God, to accomplish the great scheme of restitution, spoken of by all the Holy Prophets since the world began, the end of which is the dispensation of the fulness of times. In the which, all things shall be fulfilled, that have been spoken of since the word was made. Now the question is, unto whom is this dispensation to be given? or by whom to be revealed? The answer is, to the deliverer that was to have come out of Zion, and given to him by the angel of God. Rev. 14:7. "And I saw another angel flying in the midst of Heaven, having the everlasting gospel to preach to them that dwell on the earth, and to every nation, kindred, tongue and people, saying with a loud voice, fear God, and give glory to him for the hour of his judgement is come; worship him, that made heaven, and earth, and sea, and the fountains of water." Now observe, this angel delivers the gospel to man on the earth, and that too when the hour of the judgements of God had come on the generation, in the which the Lord should set his hand the second time, as stated above. Now we have learned that this deliverer must be clothed with the power of all the other dispensations, or it could not be called the fulness of times, for this is what it means, that all things shall be revealed, both in Heaven and on earth. For the Lord said, there was nothing secret that should not be revealed, or hid that should not come abroad, and be proclaimed upon the housetop. And this may, with propriety, be called the fulness of times. The authority connected with the ordinances, renders the time very desirable to the man of God, and renders him happy, amidst all his trials, and afflictions. To such a one, through the grace of God, we are indebted for this dispensation, as given by the angel of the Lord. But to what tribe of Israel was it to be given? We answer, to Ephraim, because to him were the greater blessings given. For the Lord said through his father, Joseph: "A seer shall the Lord raise up of the fruit of my loins; yea, he truly said; Thus saith the Lord, a choice Seer will I raise up out of the fruit of thy loins, and he shall be esteemed highly; and unto him will I give commandment, that he shall do a work for the fruit of thy loins his brethren, which shall be of great worth unto them, even to the bringing of them, to the knowledge of the covenants which I made with their fathers. And I will give unto him a commandment that he shall do no other work, save the work which I shall command him; and I will make him great in mine eyes, for he shall do my work, and he shall be great like unto

Moses; and out of weakness he shall be made strong, in that day when my work shall commence among all people, unto the restoring of the house of Israel, saith the Lord."

And thus prophesied Joseph, saying, "Behold, that seer will the Lord bless, and they that seek to destroy him shall be confounded. Behold, I am sure of the fulfillment of this promise, and his name shall be called after me; and it shall be after the name of his father; and he shall be like unto me, for the thing which the Lord shall bring forth by his hand by the power of the Father, shall bring my people unto salvation." Thus prophesied Joseph—"I am sure of this thing, even as I am sure of the promise of Moses." 2nd Book of Nephi, 2nd chapter.

And again, Jesus says, as recorded in the Book of Mormon, 526th page, 2nd edition: "Behold my servant shall deal prudently; he shall be exalted, and shall be esteemed, and be very high. As many as were astonished at thee, so shall he sprinkle many nations. Kings shall shut their mouths at him, for that which had been told them shall they see; and that which they had not heard shall they consider."

Upon this servant is bestowed the keys of the dispensation of the fullness of times. That from him, the Priesthood of God, through our Lord Jesus Christ, might be given to many, and the order of this dispensation established on the earth. And to the church he has said by commandment—(See Book of Covenants, 46th section, 2nd paragraph) "Wherefore, meaning the church, thou shalt give heed unto all his words, and commandments, which he shall give unto you as he receiveth them, walking in all holiness before me; for his word ye shall receive as from mine own mouth; in all patience and faith, for by doing these things the gates of hell shall not prevail against you." Now, my readers, you can see in some degree, the grace given unto this man of God to uswards. That we, by the great mercy of God, should receive from under his hand, the gospel of Jesus Christ, and having the promise of partaking of the fruit of the vine, on the earth with him, and with the holy prophets and patriarchs, our fathers. For these holy men are angels now. And these are they, who make the fullness of times complete with us. And they who sin against this authority given to him (the before mentioned man of God) sin not against him only, but against Moroni, who holds the keys of the stick of Ephraim. And also against Elias, who holds the keys of the bringing to pass the restitution of all things. And also John, the son of Zacharias, which Zacharias Elias visited, and gave promise that he should have a son, and his name should be John, and he should be filled with the spirit of Elias, "which John I have sent unto you, my servant Joseph Smith and Oliver Cowdery, to ordain you to this first Priesthood even as Aaron," and also Elijah who holds the keys of committing the power, to turn the hearts of the fathers to the children, and the hearts of the children to the fathers, that the whole earth may not be smitten with a curse. And also Joseph, and Jacob, and Isaac, and Abraham, your fathers, by whom the promises remain. And also Michael or Adam, the father of all, the Prince of all, the Ancient of Days. And also "Peter and James and John, whom I have sent unto you, by whom I have ordained you, and confirmed you to be apostles, and especial witnesses of my name, and bear the keys of your ministry, and of the same things I revealed unto you: unto whom I have committed the keys of my kingdom, and a dispensation of the gospel for the last time, and for the fullness of times, in the which I will gather together in one all things, both which are in heaven and which are on earth."

Therefore, brethren, beware concerning yourselves, that you sin not against the authority of this dispensation, nor think lightly of those whom God has counted worthy of so great a calling, and for whose sake he hath made them servants unto you, that you might be made heirs of God, to inherit so great a blessing, and be prepared for the grand assembly, and sit there with the ancient of days, even Adam, our father, who shall come to prepare you for the coming of Jesus Christ, our Lord: for the time is at hand, therefore, gather up your effects and gather together upon the land which the Lord has appointed for your safety.

David W. Patten

The summer of 1838, found the Saints gathered into Far West, and located in the surrounding settlements, to the number of not less than twelve thousand souls. The old spirit of mobocracy began to show itself again. An occasion was afforded for an outbreak by the August election at Gallatin in Caldwell County, where the Saints were unlawfully prevented from voting. From that time forward until their banishment from the State the following winter, the Saints in the outlying settlements and on their farms, were kept in constant fear. Bands of lawless men roamed the country over, destroying crops, burning houses, ravishing women, and driving the objects of their hatred into Far West, their only place of safety.

Wherever assistance or defense was needed, Apostle David W. Patten was to the rescue among the foremost, and his bravery soon won for him the title of "Captain Fear Not." In his presence the oppressed found a champion, and at his approach the wicked were filled with terror.

About the middle of October David was placed in command of nearly sixty men, and ordered to disperse a mob in the vicinity of Gallatin. Of this expedition it is recorded:

"When Patten's company came in sight of Gallatin, he found a body of the mob, about one hundred strong, who were amusing themselves by mocking, and in various ways tantalizing a number of the Saints whom they had captured. Seeing the approach of Patten's men, and knowing the determination of the leader, the mob broke and ran in the greatest confusion, leaving their prisoners behind them."

Probably the last manifestation of David's power with the Lord, at any rate the last of which any account is given, occurred about this time.

With others he had gone to the relief of an isolated family in the line of the mob's course, and had found the mother with several children homeless and destitute. Painfully the party were making their way on foot to Far West across the prairie, when from the fright she had received, the mother, in a delicate condition before, was threatened with severe sickness. To add to the distressing situation, a heavy storm seemed impending and the rain commenced to descend.

Always full of sympathy for the sorrowing, David at once called the party to a momentary halt, and, stepping aside into the tall grass, he commanded the storm to cease until the woman should be conveyed to a place of shelter.

Immediately, it is related, the rain was stayed, the sky began to clear, and the party went forward to their destination without further hindrance or discomfort.

Of the terrible conditions now confronting the Church Bishop Orson F. Whitney writes:

"The fall and winter of 1838, was one of the darkest periods of Church history. Mobocracy on one hand, and apostasy on the other, dealt the cause of God cruel blows, such as no human work could have hoped to withstand. The tempest of persecution, briefly lulled, burst forth with tenfold fury; no longer a city or county — a whole State rose in arms against God's people, bent upon their destruction. 'The dogs of war' were loosed upon the helpless Saints, and murder and rapine held high carnival amid the smoking ruins of peaceful homes and ravaged fields.

"Then fell the mask from the face of hypocrisy. Treason betrayed itself. Apostles, Presidents, and Elders fell from the faith and joined hands with the robbers and murderers of their brethren. Satan laughed! The very mouth of hell seemed opening to engulf the Kingdom which He who cannot lie has sworn shall stand forever."

We quote President George Q. Cannon:

"Unable to bear the pressure and to face the terrors of the times, Thomas B. Marsh had apostatized and had joined with McLellin and other evil men to act the part of Judas against the Prophet. The faith of others also failed, and, thinking by apostasy to save themselves from the destruction which seemed impending, they came out against Joseph and the Church and went over to their enemies."

Such was the condition of the Church, when Apostle David W. Patten, then the senior member and President of the Quorum of the Twelve Apostles, performed the last heroic act of his noble career.

CHAPTER VIII

His last call to arms — Battle of Crooked river — David mortally wounded — The closing scene — Wilford Woodruff's testimony — Testimony of the Prophet Joseph — His place behind the veil revealed.

On the 24th of October, a messenger came into Far West bringing news of a band of invaders under command of Rev. Samuel Bogart, who had boasted that, if he had good luck in meeting Neil Gillum, another mobocrat leader, he would give Far West thunder and lightning before noon next day. Joseph Holbrook and David Judah were at once dispatched to watch the movements of the despoilers. Near midnight these brethren returned, and reported that the mob, after plundering the house of Father Pinkham, west of the city, had made prisoners of Nathan Pinkham, William Seely and Addison Green, whom they had declared their intentions to kill that night.

"On hearing the report," the Prophet Joseph Smith records, "Judge Higbee, the first Judge of the county, ordered Lieutenant Colonel Hinkle, the highest officer in command in Far West, to send out a company to disperse the mob and retake their prisoners whom it was reported, they intended to murder that night.

"The trumpet sounded, and the brethren were assembled on the Public Square about midnight, when the facts were stated, and about seventy-five volunteered to obey the Judge's order, under command of David W. Patten, who immediately commenced their march on horseback, hoping to surprise and scatter the camp, retake the prisoners, and prevent the attack threatened upon Far West, without the loss of blood."

Apostle Parley P. Pratt, who was among the volunteers, thus graphically describes that midnight march:

"The company was soon under way, having to ride through extensive prairies, a distance of some twelve miles. The night was dark, the distant plains far and wide were illuminated by blazing fires, immense columns of smoke were seen rising in awful majesty, as if the world was on fire. This scene of grandeur can only be comprehended by those acquainted with the scenes of prairie burning; as the fire sweeps over millions of acres of dry grass in the fall season, and leaves a smooth surface divested of all vegetation.

"A thousand meteors blazing in the distance like the camp fires of some war host, threw a fitful gleam of light upon the distant sky, which many might have mistaken for the Aurora Borealis. This scene, added to the silence of the midnight, the rumbling sound of the tramping steeds, over the hard and dried surface of the plain, the clanking of the swords in their scabbards, the occasional gleam of bright armour in the flickering firelight, the gloom of surrounding darkness, and the unknown destiny of the expedition, or even of the people who sent it forth all combined to impress the mind with deep and solemn thought, and to throw a romantic vision over the imagination, which is not often experienced, except in the poet's dream, or in the wild imagery of sleeping fancy.

"In this solemn procession we moved on for some two hours, when it was supposed we were in the neighborhood of danger."

Dismounting here the company tied their horses to the field fence of Randolph McDonald, and, leaving a few men to guard the horses, proceeded on foot across the country by three different routes to the "Field house," where it was thought the mob were encamped. David, with a third of the party, took the way around the field to the right, sending Apostle Charles C. Rich, in charge of another company, to the left; while a third, under James Durfee, went directly across. All were to meet at the house of Mr. Field and take the enemy by surprise. When the forces reached the point of meeting, however, no foe was in sight.

It was now concluded that the mob must have camped at the ford below on Crooked river, and after a short exhortation from Captain Patten to trust in the Lord for victory, a march was ordered along the road to that point. As the party neared the river in the early morning just at day-break, a voice was heard calling, "Who comes there?" and at the same instant a shot was fired, when a young man, P. O'Bannion, reeled and fell from the ranks mortally wounded. Captain Patten at once ordered a charge and the company rushed forward only to see two men, who had been on guard, running into the camp of the enemy on the river bank below. Immediately all was confusion in the camp, but it was still so dark that nothing could be seen with distinctness by the brethren looking to the west, while their forms could be clearly outlined in the eastern light by the mob, who were soon in position behind the river bank below. David had just ranged his company in line, not more than fifty yards from the camp, when a deadly fire was opened upon them from behind the embankment. An answering fire was immediately ordered and with the watch-word "God and liberty," on his lips, David, ordering a charge, ran forward.

The mob fled in confusion before the rush that followed and the field was quickly won; but as David led the pursuit down the river bank, a mobber who had taken refuge behind a tree for a momentary pause before taking to the river, turned and shot him in the abdomen.

The mob routed, his brethren gathered about their wounded leader in deepest sorrow, and everything possible was done to minister to his comfort. Word was dispatched to Far West for medical assistance to meet the party, the wagons of the mob were pressed into service, and the victorious, but sorrow-stricken company took up their dreary march toward Far West. Seven of the brethren were wounded, and one, Gideon Carter, had been killed outright.

After riding a few miles in a wagon, David's suffering became so intense he was placed on a litter and carded by his brethren.

Without delay, on receiving the mournful intelligence, the Prophet Joseph Smith with his brother Hyrum, Apostle Heber C. Kimball and Elder Amasa M. Lyman, with others, as also David's grief-stricken wife, made all haste to meet the sorrowful cavalcade.

President Heber C. Kimball describes the closing scene:

"Immediately on receiving the intelligence that Brother Patten was wounded, I hastened to see him and found him in great pain, but still he was glad to see me; he was conveyed about four miles to the house of Brother

Stephen Winchester; during his removal his sufferings were so excruciating that he frequently desired us to lay him down that he might die; but being desirous to get him out of the reach of the mob, we prevailed upon him to let us carry him among his friends. We carried him on a kind of bier, fixed up from poles.

"Although he had medical assistance, his wound was such that there was no hope entertained of his recovery, and this he was perfectly aware of. In this situation, while the shades of time were lowering, and eternity with all its realities opening to his view, he bore a strong testimony to the truth of the work of the Lord, and the religion he had espoused. He was perfectly sensible and collected until he breathed his last, which occurred at about ten o'clock in the evening. Stephen Winchester, Brother Patten's wife, Bathsheba W. Bigler, with several of her father's family were present at David's death.

"The principles of the Gospel which were so precious to him before, afforded him that support and consolation at the time of his departure, which deprived death of its sting and horror. Speaking of those who had fallen from their steadfastness, he exclaimed, 'O that they were in my situation! For I feel that I have kept the faith, I have finished my course, henceforth there is laid up for me a crown, which the Lord, the righteous Judge, will give me.' Speaking to his beloved wife, he said, 'Whatever you do else, O do not deny the faith.' He all the time expressed a great desire to depart. I said to him, 'Brother David, when you get home, I want you to remember me.' He replied, 'I will.' At this time his sight was gone. A few minutes before he died, he prayed as follows, 'Father, I ask Thee in the name of Jesus Christ, that thou wouldst release my spirit, and receive it unto Thyself.' And he then said to those who surrounded his dying bed, 'Brethren, you have held me by your faith, but do give me up, and let me go, I beseech you.' We accordingly committed him to God, and he soon breathed his last, and slept in Jesus without a groan.

"This was the death of one who was an honor to the Church, and, a blessing to the Saints; and whose faith, virtue and diligence in the cause of truth will be had in remembrance by the Church of Jesus Christ from generation to generation. It was a painful way to be deprived of the labors of this worthy servant of Christ, and it cast a gloom upon the Saints; yet the glorious and sealing testimony which he bore of his acceptance with heaven and the truth of the Gospel was a matter of joy and satisfaction, not only to his immediate friends, but to the Saints at large."

Of the death of his friend, President Wilford Woodruff writes:

"Thus fell the noble David W. Patten as a martyr for the cause of God and he will receive a martyr's crown. He was valiant in the testimony of Jesus Christ while he lived upon the earth. He was a man of great faith and the power of God was with him. He was brave to a fault, even too brave to be preserved. He apparently had no fear of man about him.

"Many of the sick were healed and devils cast out under his administration."

In closing his account of the tragedy, the Prophet Joseph says:

"Brother David W. Patten was a very worthy man, beloved by all good men who knew him. He was one of the Twelve Apostles, and died as he lived, a man of God, and strong in the faith of a glorious resurrection, in a world where mobs will have no power or place."

With David's wish, formerly expressed to him, to die as a martyr, no doubt in mind, the Prophet Joseph, at the funeral on October 27, 1838, pointing to his lifeless body, testified:

"There lies a man that has done just as he said he would — he has laid down his life for his friends."

And one mightier has said:

"Greater love hath no man than this, that a man lay down his life for his friend."

A fit ending of a glorious career!

The remains were laid to rest with military honors at Far West, and the grave is now unmarked and unknown, but of the noble spirit, the Lord, in a revelation a few years subsequent to his departure, vouchsafed this intelligence:

"David Patten I have taken unto myself; behold, his Priesthood no man taketh from him; but verily I say unto you, another may be appointed unto the same calling."

And again, in speaking of Lyman Wight, who succeeded David in the Apostleship, the Lord says:

"That when he shall finish his work, that I may receive him unto myself, even as I did my servant David Patten, who is with me at this time."

If, then, to repeat, we say that great men are the Lord's object lessons to the world by whom He holds out to mankind the truths committed to their generation, what of the life before us?

From the time David heard of the Gospel, his earnest nature entered with full purpose of heart upon the work he was sent from the courts on high to perform, his whole soul was given over to faithfully bearing the message of his life:

GOD GIVES US ALL THE POWER WE HAVE,

and though in the one desire to give his life as a martyr, it may be said he fell short of the ideal:

THY WILL NOT MINE BE DONE;

yet, without a doubt, in making up the roll of his noble and great ones, Time will place next to those of the Prophet and Patriarch martyrs, Joseph and Hyrum Smith, the name of the first Apostolic martyr, David W. Patten.